The
Celebration
and
Blessing
of the
Marriage
of

____

and

____

✠

Declaration of Intention
for Marriage

NOTE: Canon I.18.4 requires couples to sign this Declaration of Intention prior to the solemnization of their marriage.

We understand the teaching of the Church that God's purpose for our marriage is for our mutual joy, for the help and comfort we will give to each other in prosperity and adversity, and, when it is God's will, for the gift and heritage of children and their nurture in the knowledge and love of God. We also understand that our marriage is to be unconditional, mutual, exclusive, faithful, and lifelong; and we engage to make the utmost effort to accept these gifts and fulfill these duties, with the help of God and the support of our community.

____

SIGNATURE

____

SIGNATURE

____

DATE

THE CELEBRATION AND BLESSING OF A MARRIAGE II

*Conforming to
the General Convention 2024*

Concerning the Service

At least one of the parties must be a baptized Christian; the ceremony must be attested by at least two witnesses; and the marriage must conform to the laws of the State and the canons of this Church.

A priest or a bishop normally presides at the Celebration and Blessing of a Marriage, because such ministers alone have the function of pronouncing the nuptial blessing, and of celebrating the Holy Eucharist.

When both a bishop and a priest are present and officiating, the bishop should pronounce the blessing and preside at the Eucharist.

A deacon, or an assisting priest, may deliver the charge, ask for the Declaration of Consent, read the Gospel, and perform other assisting functions at the Eucharist.

Where it is permitted by civil law that deacons may perform marriages, and no priest or bishop is available, a deacon may use the service which follows, omitting the nuptial blessing which follows The Prayers.

It is desirable that the Lessons from the Old Testament and the Epistles be read by lay persons.

In the opening exhortation, the full names of the persons to be married are declared. Subsequently, only their Christian names are used.

Additional Directions are on p. 25.

The Celebration and Blessing of a Marriage II

At the time appointed, the persons to be married, with their witnesses, assemble in the church or some other appropriate place.

During their entrance, a hymn, psalm, or anthem may be sung, or instrumental music may be played.

Then the Celebrant, facing the people and the persons to be married, addresses the congregation and says

Dearly beloved: We have come together in the presence of God to witness and bless the joining together of N.______________ and N.________________ in Holy Matrimony. The joining of two people in a life of mutual fidelity signifies to us the mystery of the union between Christ and his Church, and so it is worthy of being honored among all people.

The union of two people in heart, body, and mind is intended by God for their mutual joy; for the help and comfort given one another in prosperity and adversity; and, when it is God's will, for the gift of children and their nurture in the knowledge and love of the Lord. Therefore marriage is not to be entered into unadvisedly or lightly, but reverently, deliberately, and in accordance with the purposes for which it was instituted by God.

Into this holy union N.N.___________________________

________________ and N.N._______________________

_____________________ now come to be joined.

If any of you can show just cause why they may not lawfully be married, speak now; or else for ever hold your peace.

Then the Celebrant says to the persons to be married

I require and charge you both, here in the presence of God, that if either of you knows any reason why you may not be united in marriage lawfully, and in accordance with God's Word, you do now confess it.

The Declaration of Consent

The Celebrant says to one member of the couple, then to the other

N.__________________________________, will you have this *woman/man/person* to be your *wife/husband/spouse*; to live together in the covenant of marriage? Will you love *her/him*, comfort *her/him*, honor and keep *her/him*, in sickness and in health, and, forsaking all others, be faithful to *her/him* as long as you both shall live?

Answer

I will.

The Celebrant then addresses the congregation, saying

Will all of you witnessing these promises do all in your power to uphold these two persons in their marriage?

People

We will.

If there is to be a presentation or a giving in marriage, it takes place at this time. See Additional Directions, p. 25.

A hymn, psalm, or anthem may follow.

The Ministry of the Word

The Celebrant then says to the people

The Lord be with you.

People

And also with you.

Celebrant

Let us pray.

O gracious and everliving God, you have created humankind in your image: Look mercifully upon N._____________ and N._____________ who come to you seeking your blessing, and assist them with your grace, that with true fidelity and steadfast love they may honor and keep the promises and vows they make; through Jesus Christ our Savior, who lives and reigns with you in the unity of the Holy Spirit, one God, for ever and ever. *Amen.*

> *Then one or more of the following passages from Holy Scripture is read. Other readings from Scripture suitable for the occasion may be used. If there is to be a Communion, a passage from the Gospel always concludes the Readings.*

> Genesis 1:26-28 (Male and female he created them)
> Song of Solomon 2:10-13; 8:6-7 (Many waters cannot quench love)
> Tobit 8:5b-8 (*New English Bible*) (That she and I may grow old together)
> 1 Corinthians 13:1-13 (Love is patient and kind)
> Ephesians 3:14-19 (The Father from whom every family is named)

Ephesians 5:1-2 (Walk in love, as Christ loved us)
Colossians 3:12-17 (Love which binds everything together in
    harmony)
1 John 4:7-16 (Let us love one another for love is of God)

*Between the Readings, a psalm, hymn, or anthem may be sung
or said. Appropriate psalms are Psalm 67, Psalm 127, and
Psalm 128.*

*When a passage from the Gospel is to be read, all stand, and the
Deacon or Minister appointed says*

The Holy Gospel of our Lord Jesus Christ according to

______________________________.

People

Glory to you, Lord Christ.

Matthew 5:1-10 (The Beatitudes)
Matthew 5:13-16 (You are the light . . . Let your light so shine)
Matthew 7:21, 24-29 (Like a wise man who built his house
    upon the rock)
John 15:9-12 (Love one another as I have loved you)

After the Gospel, the Reader says

The Gospel of the Lord.

People

Praise to you, Lord Christ.

A homily or other response to the Readings may follow.

The Marriage

Each member of the couple, in turn, takes the right hand of the other and says

In the Name of God, I, N.________________, take you, N.________________, to be my *wife/husband/spouse*, to have and to hold from this day forward, for better for worse, for richer for poorer, in sickness and in health, to love and to cherish, until we are parted by death. This is my solemn vow.

The Priest may ask God's blessing on rings as follows

Bless, O Lord, *these rings* to be *signs* of the vows by which N.________________ and N.________________ have bound themselves to each other; through Jesus Christ our Lord. *Amen.*

The giver places the ring on the ring finger of the other's hand and says

N.________________, I give you this ring as a symbol of my vow, and with all that I am, and all that I have, I honor you, in the Name of the Father, and of the Son, and of the Holy Spirit (*or* in the Name of God).

Then the Celebrant joins the right hands of the couple and says

Now that N.________________ and N.________________ have given themselves to each other by solemn vows, with the joining of hands and the giving and receiving of *rings*, I pronounce that they are wed to one another, in the Name of the Father, and of the Son, and of the Holy Spirit. Those whom God has joined together let no one put asunder. *Amen.*

The Prayers

All standing, the Celebrant says

Let us pray together in the words our Savior taught us.

People and Celebrant

Our Father, who art in heaven,
    hallowed be thy Name,
    thy kingdom come,
    thy will be done,
       on earth as it is in heaven.
Give us this day our daily bread.
And forgive us our trespasses,
    as we forgive those
       who trespass against us.
And lead us not into temptation,
    but deliver us from evil.
For thine is the kingdom,
    and the power, and the glory,
    for ever and ever. *Amen.*

Our Father in heaven,
    hallowed be your Name,
    your kingdom come,
    your will be done,
       on earth as in heaven.
Give us today our daily bread.
Forgive us our sins
    as we forgive those
       who sin against us.
Save us from the time of trial,
    and deliver us from evil.
For the kingdom, the power,
    and the glory are yours,
    now and for ever. *Amen.*

If Communion is to follow, the Lord's Prayer may be omitted here.

The Deacon or other person appointed reads the following prayers, to which the People respond, saying, Amen.

If there is not to be a Communion, one or more of the prayers may be omitted.

Let us pray.

Eternal God, creator and preserver of all life, author of salvation, and giver of all grace: Look with favor upon the world you have made, and for which your Son gave his life, and especially upon N._________________ and N._________________ whom you make one flesh in Holy Matrimony. *Amen.*

Give them wisdom and devotion in the ordering of their common life, that each may be to the other a strength in need, a counselor in perplexity, a comfort in sorrow, and a companion in joy. *Amen.*

Grant that their wills may be so knit together in your will, and their spirits in your Spirit, that they may grow in love and peace with you and one another all the days of their life. *Amen.*

Give them grace, when they hurt each other, to recognize and acknowledge their fault, and to seek each other's forgiveness and yours. *Amen.*

Make their life together a sign of Christ's love to this sinful and broken world, that unity may overcome estrangement, forgiveness heal guilt, and joy conquer despair. *Amen.*

Bestow on them, if it is your will, the gift and heritage of children, and the grace to bring them up to know you, to love you, and to serve you. *Amen.*

Give them such fulfillment of their mutual affection that they may reach out in love and concern for others. *Amen.*

Grant that all married persons who have witnessed these vows may find their lives strengthened and their loyalties confirmed. *Amen.*

Grant that the bonds of our common humanity, by which all your children are united one to another, and the living to the dead, may be so transformed by your grace, that your will may be done on earth as it is in heaven; where, O Father, with your Son and the Holy Spirit, you live and reign in perfect unity, now and for ever. *Amen.*

The Blessing of the Marriage

The people remain standing. The couple kneel, and the Priest says one of the following prayers

Most gracious God, we give you thanks for your tender love in sending Jesus Christ to come among us, to be born of a human mother, and to make the way of the cross to be the way of life. We thank you, also, for consecrating the union of two people in his Name. By the power of your Holy Spirit, pour out the abundance of your blessing upon

N.________________ and N.________________ . Defend them from every enemy. Lead them into all peace. Let their love for each other be a seal upon their hearts, a mantle about their shoulders, and a crown upon their foreheads. Bless them in their work and in their companionship; in their sleeping and in their waking; in their joys and in their sorrows; in their life and in their death. Finally, in your mercy, bring them to that table where your saints feast for ever in your heavenly home; through Jesus Christ our Lord, who with you and the Holy Spirit lives and reigns, one God, for ever and ever. *Amen.*

or this

O God, you have so consecrated the covenant of marriage that in it is represented the spiritual unity between Christ and his Church: Send therefore your blessing upon these your servants, that they may so love, honor, and cherish each other in faithfulness and patience, in wisdom and true godliness, that their home may be a haven of blessing and peace; through Jesus Christ our Lord, who lives and reigns with you and the Holy Spirit, one God, now and for ever. *Amen.*

The couple still kneeling, the Priest adds this blessing

God the Father, God the Son, God the Holy Spirit, bless, preserve, and keep you; the Lord mercifully with his favor look upon you, and fill you with all spiritual benediction and grace; that you may faithfully live together in this life, and in the age to come have life everlasting. *Amen.*

The Peace

The Celebrant may say to the people

The peace of the Lord be always with you.

People

And also with you.

The newly married couple then greet each other, after which greetings may be exchanged throughout the congregation.

When Communion is not to follow, the wedding party leaves the church. A hymn, psalm, or anthem may be sung; or instrumental music may be played.

At the Eucharist

The liturgy continues with the Offertory, at which the newly married couple may present the offerings of bread and wine.

The Holy Communion

The Celebrant may begin the Offertory with one of the sentences on p. 376 in the Book of Common Prayer, *or with some other sentence of Scripture.*

During the Offertory, a hymn, psalm, or anthem may be sung.

Representatives of the congregation bring the people's offerings of bread and wine, and money or other gifts, to the deacon or celebrant. The people stand while the offerings are presented and placed on the Altar.

The Great Thanksgiving

Alternative forms will be found on p. 367 in the Book of Common Prayer, *and following.*

Eucharistic Prayer A

The people remain standing. The Celebrant, whether bishop or priest, faces them and sings or says

The Lord be with you.

People

And also with you.

Celebrant

Lift up your hearts.

People

We lift them to the Lord.

Celebrant

Let us give thanks to the Lord our God.

People

It is right to give him thanks and praise.

Then, facing the Holy Table, the Celebrant proceeds

It is right, and a good and joyful thing, always and every-where to give thanks to you, Father Almighty, Creator of heaven and earth.

Here a Proper Preface is sung or said on all Sundays, and on other occasions as appointed. See below, p. 26.

Therefore we praise you, joining our voices with Angels and Archangels and with all the company of heaven, who for ever sing this hymn to proclaim the glory of your Name:

Celebrant and People

Holy, holy, holy Lord, God of power and might, heaven and earth are full of your glory.
  Hosanna in the highest.
Blessed is he who comes in the name of the Lord.
  Hosanna in the highest.

The people stand or kneel.

Then the Celebrant continues

Holy and gracious Father: In your infinite love you made us for yourself; and, when we had fallen into sin and become subject to evil and death, you, in your mercy, sent Jesus Christ, your only and eternal Son, to share our human nature, to live and die as one of us, to reconcile us to you, the God and Father of all.

He stretched out his arms upon the cross, and offered himself, in obedience to your will, a perfect sacrifice for the whole world.

> *At the following words concerning the bread, the Celebrant is to hold it, or lay a hand upon it; and at the words concerning the cup, to hold or place a hand upon the cup and any other vessel containing wine to be consecrated.*

On the night he was handed over to suffering and death, our Lord Jesus Christ took bread; and when he had given thanks to you, he broke it, and gave it to his disciples, and said, "Take, eat: This is my Body, which is given for you. Do this for the remembrance of me."

After supper he took the cup of wine; and when he had given thanks, he gave it to them, and said, "Drink this, all of you: This is my Blood of the new Covenant, which is shed for you and for many for the forgiveness of sins. Whenever you drink it, do this for the remembrance of me."

Therefore we proclaim the mystery of faith:

> *Celebrant and People*

Christ has died.
Christ is risen.
Christ will come again.

> *The Celebrant continues*

We celebrate the memorial of our redemption, O Father, in this sacrifice of praise and thanksgiving. Recalling his death, resurrection, and ascension, we offer you these gifts.

Sanctify them by your Holy Spirit to be for your people the Body and Blood of your Son, the holy food and drink of new and unending life in him. Sanctify us also that we may faithfully receive this holy Sacrament, and serve you in unity, constancy, and peace; and at the last day bring us with all your saints into the joy of your eternal kingdom.

All this we ask through your Son Jesus Christ. By him, and with him, and in him, in the unity of the Holy Spirit all honor and glory is yours, Almighty Father, now and for ever. *Amen.*

And now, as our Savior
Christ has taught us,
we are bold to say,

As our Savior Christ
has taught us,
we now pray,

People and Celebrant

Our Father, who art in heaven,
    hallowed be thy Name,
    thy kingdom come,
    thy will be done,
        on earth as it is in heaven.
Give us this day our daily bread.
And forgive us our trespasses,
    as we forgive those
        who trespass against us.
And lead us not into temptation,
    but deliver us from evil.
For thine is the kingdom,
    and the power, and the glory,
    for ever and ever. *Amen.*

Our Father in heaven,
    hallowed be your Name,
    your kingdom come,
    your will be done,
        on earth as in heaven.
Give us today our daily bread.
Forgive us our sins
    as we forgive those
        who sin against us.
Save us from the time of trial,
    and deliver us from evil.
For the kingdom, the power,
    and the glory are yours,
    now and for ever. *Amen.*

The Breaking of the Bread

The Celebrant breaks the consecrated Bread.

A period of silence is kept.

Then may be sung or said

[Alleluia.] Christ our Passover is sacrificed for us; *Therefore let us keep the feast.* [*Alleluia.*]

> *In Lent, Alleluia is omitted, and may be omitted at other times except during Easter Season.*

> *In place of, or in addition to, the preceding, some other suitable anthem may be used.*

> *Facing the people, the Celebrant says the following Invitation*

The Gifts of God for the People of God.

> *and may add*

Take them in remembrance that Christ died for you, and feed on him in your hearts by faith, with thanksgiving.

> *The ministers receive the Sacrament in both kinds, and then immediately deliver it to the people.*

> *At the Communion, it is appropriate that the newly married couple receive Communion first, after the ministers.*

> *The Bread and the Cup are given to the communicants with these words*

The Body (Blood) of our Lord Jesus Christ keep you in everlasting life. [*Amen.*]

> *or with these words*

The Body of Christ, the bread of heaven. [*Amen.*] The Blood of Christ, the cup of salvation. [*Amen.*]

> *During the ministration of Communion, hymns, psalms, or anthems may be sung.*

> *When necessary, the Celebrant consecrates additional bread and wine, using the form on p. 408 in the* Book of Common Prayer.

After Communion, the Celebrant says

Let us pray.

Celebrant and People

In place of the usual postcommunion prayer, the following is said

O God, the giver of all that is true and lovely and gracious: We give you thanks for binding us together in these holy mysteries of the Body and Blood of your Son Jesus Christ.

Grant that by your Holy Spirit, N.______________________ and N.______________________, now joined in Holy Matrimony, may become one in heart and soul, live in fidelity and peace, and obtain those eternal joys prepared for all who love you; for the sake of Jesus Christ our Lord. *Amen.*

The Bishop when present, or the Priest, may bless the people. The Deacon, or the Celebrant, dismisses them with these words

Let us go forth in the name of Christ.

People

Thanks be to God.

or this

Deacon

Go in peace to love and serve the Lord.

People

Thanks be to God.

or this

Deacon

Let us go forth into the world,
rejoicing in the power of the Spirit.

People

Thanks be to God.

or this

Deacon

Let us bless the Lord.

People

Thanks be to God.

From the Easter Vigil through the Day of Pentecost "Alleluia, Alleluia" may be added to any of the dismissals.

The People respond

Thanks be to God. Alleluia, Alleluia.

As the wedding party leaves the church, a hymn, psalm, or anthem may be sung; or instrumental music may be played.

The Blessing of a Civil Marriage II

The rite begins as prescribed for celebrations of the Holy Eucharist, using the Collect and Lessons appointed in the Marriage service.

After the Gospel (and homily), the couple stand before the Celebrant, who addresses them in these or similar words

N.__________________ and N.__________________, you have come here today to seek the blessing of God and of his Church upon your marriage. I require, therefore, that you promise, with the help of God, to fulfill the obligations which Christian Marriage demands.

The Celebrant then addresses one member of the couple, then the other, saying

N.__________________, you have taken N.__________________ to be your *wife/husband/spouse*. Do you promise to love *her/him*, comfort *her/him*, honor and keep *her/him*, in sickness and in health, and, forsaking all others, to be faithful to *her/him* as long as you both shall live?

Answer

I do.

The Celebrant then addresses the congregation, saying

Will you who have witnessed these promises do all in your power to uphold these two persons in their marriage?

People

We will.

If rings are to be blessed, the members of the couple extend their hands toward the Priest [or Bishop], who says

Bless, O Lord, *these rings* to be *signs* of the vows by which N._______________ and N._______________ have bound themselves to each other; through Jesus Christ our Lord. *Amen.*

The Celebrant joins the right hands of the couple and says

Those whom God has joined together let no one put asunder.

People

Amen.

The service continues with The Prayers on p. 10.

An Order for Marriage II

If it is desired to celebrate a marriage otherwise than as provided in the Book of Common Prayer *or any authorized alternative thereto, this Order is used.*

Normally, the celebrant is a priest or bishop. Where permitted by civil law, and when no priest or bishop is available, a deacon may function as celebrant, but does not pronounce a nuptial blessing.

The laws of the State and the canons of this Church having been complied with, the couple, together with their witnesses, families, and friends assemble in the church or in some other convenient place.

1. The teaching of the Church concerning Holy Matrimony, as it is declared in the formularies and canons of this Church, is briefly stated.

2. The intention of the two to enter the state of matrimony, and their free consent, is publicly ascertained.

3. One or more Readings, one of which is always from Holy Scripture, may precede the exchange of vows. If there is to be a Communion, a Reading from the Gospel is always included.

4. The vows are exchanged, using the following form

In the Name of God, I, N.________________________, take you, N.________________________, to be my *wife/husband/spouse*, to have and to hold from this day forward, for better for worse, for richer for poorer, in sickness and in health, to love and to cherish, until we are parted by death. This is my solemn vow.

or this

I, N.__________________, take thee, N.__________________, to my wedded *wife/husband/spouse*, to have and to hold from this day forward, for better for worse, for richer for poorer, in sickness and in health, to love and to cherish, till death us do part, according to God's holy ordinance; and thereto I plight [*or* give] thee my troth.

5. The Celebrant declares the union of the couple, in the Name of the Father, and of the Son, and of the Holy Spirit.

6. Prayers are offered for the couple, for their life together, for the Christian community, and for the world.

7. A priest or bishop pronounces a solemn blessing upon the couple.

8. If there is no Communion, the service concludes with the Peace, the couple first greeting each other. The Peace may be exchanged throughout the assembly.

9. If there is to be a Communion, the service continues with the Peace and the Offertory. The Holy Eucharist may be celebrated either according to Rite One or Rite Two, or according to the Order on p. 401 of the Book of Common Prayer.

Additional Directions

If Banns are to be published, the following form is used

I publish the Banns of Marriage between N.N._____________
of __________________ and N.N.________________ of
__________________. If any of you know just cause why
they may not be joined together in Holy Matrimony, you are
bidden to declare it. This is the first [*or* second, *or* third] time
of asking.

> The Celebration and Blessing of a Marriage II *may be used with
> any authorized liturgy for the Holy Eucharist. This service then
> replaces the Ministry of the Word, and the Eucharist begins
> with the Offertory.*

> *After the Declaration of Consent, if there is to be a giving in
> marriage, or presentation, the Celebrant asks,*

Who presents [gives] these two people to be married to each
other?

> *The appropriate answer is, "I do." If more than one person
> responds, they do so together.*

> *For the Ministry of the Word it is fitting that the couple to be
> married remain where they may conveniently hear the reading
> of Scripture. They may approach the Altar, either for the
> exchange of vows, or for the Blessing of the Marriage.*

> *It is appropriate that all remain standing until the conclusion of
> the Collect. Seating may be provided for the wedding party, so
> that all may be seated for the Lessons and the homily.*

> *The Apostles' Creed may be recited after the Lessons, or after
> the homily, if there is one.*

> *When desired, some other suitable symbol of the vows may be
> used in place of the ring.*

At the Offertory, it is desirable that the bread and wine be presented to the ministers by the newly married persons. They may then remain before the Lord's Table and receive Holy Communion before other members of the congregation.

Prefaces for Marriage

The following Proper Preface is proposed for trial use as an addition to the Prefaces for Rites One and Two, Book of Common Prayer *pp.* 349 *and* 381.

Because in the union of two people in faithful love, we are bound in joy to our Savior Christ; who in his own offering of love makes the whole creation new.

From the Catechism

These paragraphs are proposed for trial use as an amendment of the section on Holy Matrimony in An Outline of the Faith (also known as the Catechism), Book of Common Prayer *p.* 861.

Q. What is Holy Matrimony?

A. Holy Matrimony is Christian marriage, in which two people enter into a life-long union, make their vows before God and the Church, and receive the grace and blessing of God to help them fulfill their vows.

Q. What is required of those to be married?

A. It is required of those to be married that at least one member of the couple be baptized and that they have been instructed that Christian marriage is an unconditional, mutual, exclusive, faithful and lifelong commitment intended for the couple's mutual joy, for the help and comfort given to each other in prosperity and adversity, and when it is God's will, for the gift and heritage of children and their nurture in the knowledge and love of God.

Wedding Party

The Marriage Certificate

This is to Certify

THAT

____

AND

____

WERE UNITED IN

Holy Matrimony

ON ______________________________ A.D.____________

IN ____

____

ACCORDING TO THE LITURGICAL FORM AUTHORIZED
BY THE EPISCOPAL CHURCH, AND IN ACCORDANCE

WITH THE LAWS OF ______________________________

(SIGNED) ______________________________________

____

DATE ____

WITNESSES ____

____